Snowgirl

By Allyson Tidwell

Illustrated by Jean Gallagher

ISBN:1507677030
ISBN-13:9781507677032

DEDICATION

To my Grandma and Papa, I love you so much!

ACKNOWLEDGMENTS

I would like to thank my teacher, Ms. Davis, for encouraging me to write and for editing my book. Thank you.

I would also like to thank, Jean Gallagher, your pictures are amazing.

One winter morning I woke up and it was snowing

outside. I went downstairs and ate my

Breakfast. During breakfast I asked my mom if I

could build a snowgirl and she said, "Yes." I was so

happy!

I put on my hat, scarf, snow pants, jacket, snow boots, and gloves. I was dressed in my warmest clothes.

The first thing I did was make the body. Then I put on her eyes, nose, and mouth, but something was missing. She needed accessories! I put a tiara, scarf, purse, and broom on her. She looked fabulous. My snowgirl was finally complete!

I played with her for awhile, but I noticed something

else was missing. She still needed the most perfect,

absolutely amazing, positively outstanding name.

"Her name should be Princess Marie," I said.

After a while I started to get cold, very very cold. I

went inside and drank hot coco with marshmallows.

Then I realized I had missed lunch and it was time

for dinner. I had pizza for dinner and orange juice to

drink.

After dinner I watched Frosty the Snowman Returns.

I went to bed when the movie was over.

Before I turned out the lights, I looked out my window. I saw the most horrible thing in my front yard. My neighbor's cat was about to destroy my terrific snowgirl. "Oh No!" I shouted. My mom ran into my room like a speeding rocket to see what was the matter. "What's the matter?" my mom asked. The neighbor's cat is about to destroy my snowgirl! My mom looked out my window, "Oh my," she said, as she looked back at me. I said, "We have to do something to stop the neighbor's cat and save my snowgirl."

My mom helped me get dressed in my hat, scarf, boots, and coat. My mom and I ran outside, but we were too late. The neighbor's cat tore apart my snowgirl. I was crying so hard. "We are too late," I cried. I made a snowgirl for no reason.

After that my mom and I went inside my house. I

went to bed crying. I had a dream, my snowgirl was

perfect and we played for hours.

When I woke up the next morning I looked outside

and I saw a miracle! My snowgirl was magically

rebuilt. "Oh my gosh!" I said. I can not believe

what I'm seeing. I was so excited.

I skipped breakfast, put on my warmest clothes, and ran outside like an exploding rocket. I hugged my snowgirl and said, "I will never ever let the neighbor's cat attack you again."

ABOUT THE AUTHOR

ALLYSON IS A 7 YEAR OLD WITH A PASSION FOR WRITING. SHE ALSO LOVES READING AND DANCING. THIS IS HER FIRST BOOK AND THIS IS ONLY THE BEGINNING.